Samuel French Acting Edition

The Bells

by Theresa Rebeck

SAMUELFRENCH.COM   SAMUELFRENCH.CO.UK

Copyright © 2007 by Mad Woman in the Attic, Inc.
All Rights Reserved

THE BELLS is fully protected under the copyright laws of the United States of America, the British Commonwealth, including Canada, and all other countries of the Copyright Union. All rights, including professional and amateur stage productions, recitation, lecturing, public reading, motion picture, radio broadcasting, television and the rights of translation into foreign languages are strictly reserved.

ISBN 978-0-573-64247-0

www.SamuelFrench.com
www.SamuelFrench.co.uk

FOR PRODUCTION ENQUIRIES

UNITED STATES AND CANADA
Info@SamuelFrench.com
1-866-598-8449

UNITED KINGDOM AND EUROPE
Plays@SamuelFrench.co.uk
020-7255-4302

Each title is subject to availability from Samuel French, depending upon country of performance. Please be aware that *THE BELLS* may not be licensed by Samuel French in your territory. Professional and amateur producers should contact the nearest Samuel French office or licensing partner to verify availability.

CAUTION: Professional and amateur producers are hereby warned that *THE BELLS* is subject to a licensing fee. Publication of this play(s) does not imply availability for performance. Both amateurs and professionals considering a production are strongly advised to apply to Samuel French before starting rehearsals, advertising, or booking a theatre. A licensing fee must be paid whether the title(s) is presented for charity or gain and whether or not admission is charged. Professional/Stock licensing fees are quoted upon application to Samuel French.

No one shall make any changes in this title(s) for the purpose of production. No part of this book may be reproduced, stored in a retrieval system, or transmitted in any form, by any means, now known or yet to be invented, including mechanical, electronic, photocopying, recording, videotaping, or otherwise, without the prior written permission of the publisher. No one shall upload this title(s), or part of this title(s), to any social media websites.

For all enquiries regarding motion picture, television, and other media rights, please contact Samuel French.

MUSIC USE NOTE

Licensees are solely responsible for obtaining formal written permission from copyright owners to use copyrighted music in the performance of this play and are strongly cautioned to do so. If no such permission is obtained by the licensee, then the licensee must use only original music that the licensee owns and controls. Licensees are solely responsible and liable for all music clearances and shall indemnify the copyright owners of the play(s) and their licensing agent, Samuel French, against any costs, expenses, losses and liabilities arising from the use of music by licensees. Please contact the appropriate music licensing authority in your territory for the rights to any incidental music.

IMPORTANT BILLING AND CREDIT REQUIREMENTS

If you have obtained performance rights to this title, please refer to your licensing agreement for important billing and credit requirements.

All Licensees shall be required to give the following acknowledgement on the title page of all programs distributed in connection with the performance of the play:

THE BELLS was commissioned by
the Intiman Theatre Company, Seattle, WA
Bartlett Sher, Artistic Director   Laura Penn, Managing Director

THE BELLS was originally produced by
the McCarter Theatre, Princeton, NJ
Emily Mann, Artistic Director   Jeffrey Woodward, Managing Director

THE BELLS had its world premiere at the McCarter Theatre on Tuesday, March 22,, 2005, Emily Mann, Artistic Director, Jeffrey Woodward, Managing Director, in the Matthews Theatre. The production was directed by Emily Mann with the following cast and artistic staff:

XUIFEI	Pun Bandhu
JIM	Paul Butler
SALLY	Fiona Gallagher
BAPTISTE	Christopher Innvar
ANNETTE	Marin Ireland
MATHIAS	Ted Marcoux
CHARLIE	Michael McCarty

Eugene Lee – *Set Designer*
Jennifer Von Mayrhauser – *Costume Designer*
Frances Aronson – *Lighting Designer*
Darron L. West – *Sound Designer*
J. Steven White – *Fight Director*
Liz Engelman – *Dramaturg*
Mara Isaacs – *Producing Director*
Scott French – *Line Producer*
David York – *Director of Production*
Mindy Richardson – *Production Stage Manager*
Alison Cote – *Stage Manager*

CHARACTERS

XUIFEI, Chinese, 20's
JIM, African-American, late 50's-60's
SALLY, a prostitute, 30's
BAPTISTE, French-Canadian, 30's
ANNETTE, early 20's
MATHIAS, an innkeeper, 45-60
CHARLIE, a prospector, 50's

SETTING

The Yukon
1899 and 1917

ACT I

Scene 1

(XUIFEI stands alone.)

XUIFEI. I never knew the world could be so cold. In my village, when the rains came, the cold would crawl into the bamboo and sleep in the pitch of our ceiling. The rain came in and sat with us at our meals, like a sorrowful friend, and the cold spoke softly to our bones. But this is a cold so deep and wild there is no word that names it. They told me not to come here, but there was a hole in my heart and I did not know how to stay in one place. I don't want to die here. I want to die in my home, where the cold is warm.

Scene 2

(The street. JIM and SALLY throw themselves on CHARLIE, struggling to get a bottle from him.)

JIM. Give to me! Come on! Charlie, you've had enough

now—

CHARLIE. Get off, you stinking drunk—
SALLY. You bastard! Give me the damn—owwww—
CHARLIE. No! No!
JIM. Give it to me!! Give it to me!
CHARLIE *(Drinking)* Go to hell, you stinking goddamn stinking—it's my turn, I'm gonna take my damn turn, the both of you had your damn turns now it's my damn turn!
SALLY. *(Overlap)* Owww—dammit, Charlie, now you—ooоowwww—

(They roll and fight for a long moment until SALLY grabs the bottle and threatens to smash CHARLIE in the head with it.)

CHARLIE. Don't don't don't—Sally, come on, darlin'—don't—Sally! It's almost Christmas now, and Christmas is a time of year when people are kind and good to each other—
JIM. Have a little Christmas spirit, Sally—now now now, you're spilling the hootch now, Sally, honey. Now what's the point of that, darlin'. *(SALLY looks at the bottle, rights it, takes a rather long drink. The two men are ready to leap on her. She takes a step back and takes another drink. Both of them howl.)* Oh, my god—that is—now, Sally—you had your turn now!

CHARLIE. *(Overlap)* Jesus god above, you stinking greedy whore—
SALLY. I'm not a whore!
CHARLIE. Say that again, and you're a liar and a whore and a thief for that matter, stealing liquor from Mathias—
SALLY. I'm not a thief! Mathias give me this, for a Christ-

mas present!

CHARLIE. You're lying, you're a liar and a whore and a thief—

JIM. A liar and a whore and a drunk and a thief. That's like a song, isn't it? *(Singing)* Sweet Sally Maguire, a whore and a liar—

CHARLIE. A thief, when it suited her needs. Went down to the river, 'cause a man wouldn't give her—

JIM. A drink—cause she's a drunk—

SALLY. You're a drunk you stinking drunk—

JIM. You're a drunk—

SALLY. No, you're a drunk—

(They fight over the bottle again. SALLY makes off with the bottle. JIM grabs her by the ankle, yanks her back, and gets the bottle himself. It is empty.)

JIM. Goddamnit! You drunken thievin' whore!
SALLY. Least I never...

(This stops JIM in his tracks.)

JIM. What'd you say?
CHARLIE. She didn't say nothing.
SALLY. The hell I didn't.
JIM. The hell she didn't—
CHARLIE. Come on now, it's Christmas, what you want to be dragging that up for?
SALLY. *(Insistent)* Show me your palm! Show it to me!
JIM. I don't have to show you nothin' you crazy drunken whore!

CHARLIE. Come on, now! It's Christmas! Christmas is a holiday of good will and brotherhood, we're all, Christ's birth and have a drink and all.

(He pulls a couple of more bottles out of his pockets and holds them out.)

SALLY. I know what I know, Charlie—
CHARLIE. Sally. Leave it be and have a drink. We're all friends, now. This is a friendly town, not like Skagway or nothing. You remember that guy? That guy in Skagway? Jim, you remember that guy?
JIM. What guy.
CHARLIE. You know, that guy. Back in, I can't remember the year, I went there. He was running that town ragged, evil as a snake, you went in for a couple of drinks, next thing you know he was threatening to kill you over fifty cents, an old pair of boots, just a foul mood was enough to set that guy off and he had the gang to do it for him, too. Everybody smiling, talking like friends, like old friends explaining we're gonna kill you like they're asking you over for dinner or something. That's the way things were that year. So much gold in the air it made the brain go hot with fever, even in sixty below, didn't even matter there was nothing to spend it on but cheap booze and women you couldn't hardly look at, everyone running up from wherever the world spit them out to come stand in the freezing cold, the heat in their blood driving them through the Chilkoot Pass like dead men on their way to hell. Pack horses driven so hard they was jumping off the trail into the abyss, first time in my life I ever saw a horse commit suicide but that's where it took us, all of us screaming for

gold like it was gonna save you from what it meant to be human. No goddamn wonder that guy could turn a town like Skagway into our own local version of Hades.

JIM. What year was this?

CHARLIE. Don't matter. My point is, this is a friendly town! Nothing like Skagway.

(They sit for a moment.)

JIM. You hungry?

SALLY. Yeah, I'm hungry.

JIM. Maybe Mathias give us something to eat.

CHARLIE. Better hope Annie's not looking. She is, we gonna have to get Sally, with her sticky fingers, do her magic.

SALLY. She gives me a pain.

JIM. Don't talk to her. Talk to Mathias.

CHARLIE. It's Christmas, he'll give us some eggs or something.

SALLY. 'Cause I offered to work it off with him. It's not natural, livin' like a priest when there's whores in the world.

JIM. *(Singing)* Sweet Sally Maguire, she sings in the choir, and oh how the priests gather round.

CHARLIE. There's nothing quite finer than her sweet vaginer, for making that good godly sound...

(They are off.)

Scene 3

ANNETTE. Pa! Where are you, Pa! Six, seven eight—goddammit, PA! PAAAAA—they been stealing from us again, PA!!!

(ANNETTE at the inn. ANNETTE is counting bottles at the bar.)

MATHIAS. Here I am, here I am! Just went out to see the sun rise, soon as it showed over the horizon, there it goes again, back into the earth. Wind's kicking up too, snow ghosts rising out of the mountains, fading as soon as they take shape. To hell with them, I say. Go on, get out of here! Six weeks of black don't scare us! We're going to light this town! I'm telling you, it's gonna work, this place is going to burn bright as the stars themselves! So that when the heavens look out, we are what they're gonna see, this place, shining like a star, past reason and hope, brighter than all of it, shining into the night.

ANNETTE. Wait a minute. That's why you bought all those lanterns in Dawson City? To light the whole town? Oh my god, you're just going to give them all away, aren't you?

MATHIAS. I bought so many because you got to believe in the light of us, Annie, you know what it is when the darkness is all we have, we're not meant to live like that. Good lord tells us to light a candle, rather than curse the dark, that's what I'm doing. *(He lights the lamp.)* There you go. A single lamp, burning through the endless night.

ANNETTE. Not a single lamp, a whole mess of them, that you're just giving away to anybody who happens to need one—

MATHIAS. We'll put them in with the Christmas baskets.
ANNETTE. The Christmas baskets? How much is that going to run us this year? Don't tell me, I don't want to know. I want to talk to you about Sally and Charlie.
MATHIAS. Look how pretty you look. You do something different to your hair?
ANNETTE. I combed it.
MATHIAS. You should do that, more often.
ANNETTE. I counted before and now I'm counting again, and Sally and Charlie both been stealing liquor. They come in here, you make me wait on 'em, treat 'em like decent people—
MATHIAS. Their hearts are in the right place.
ANNETTE. They got no hearts! That Jim Lynch is just as bad, they're barely, there's dogs on the street more human than those three!

(He looks at her. She looks away.)

MATHIAS. Just because this place is wild doesn't mean you have to be.
ANNETTE. You tell me how to be any other way.

(There is a sad beat, then—)

MATHIAS. You're lonely, I know that.
ANNETTE. Pa, that's not—I don't want to talk about this.
MATHIAS. Annie.
ANNETTE. No, no, I'm fine. You're right, I'm just in a bad mood over nothing, I'm ashamed of myself. I'll finish cleaning this up and ... come help you with those baskets.

MATHIAS. It's all right. I can—
ANNETTE. *(Snapping)* Pa! I said I would help, would you just stop trying to take care of me all the time I'm fine I told you!
BAPTISTE. *(In doorway)* Hello?

(ANNETTE turns, furious again.)

ANNETTE. Jesus god above, what the hell are you doing? We're not open, all right?
BAPTISTE. I'm sorry.

(ANNETTE stops. He is quite handsome.)

ANNETTE. Oh. I'm sorry. I thought you were someone else.
BAPTISTE. You are not open?

(And he's French. She's speechless.)

MATHIAS. Of course we're open! Come on in, have a seat. Annie. We have a customer.

(MATHIAS gestures to her to wait on him. Nervous, suddenly, she does.)

ANNETTE. Yes, of course. Excuse me. What can I get you? I mean, can I get you anything?
BAPTISTE. Food, you have food?
ANNETTE. Any particular kind of food?
BAPTISTE. No.
ANNETTE. Okay, we have that. Anything to drink?

BAPTISTE. Wine? Do you have wine?
ANNETTE. Yes, we have that.
BAPTISTE. I would like some wine.
ANNETTE. I'll go get that then.

(ANNETTE nods, goes to the bar. MATHIAS steps forward, friendly.)

MATHIAS. You're French.
BAPTISTE. Canadian.
MATHIAS. French Canadian. Annie speaks French.
BAPTISTE. *(Interested)* Yes?
ANNETTE. *(Embarrassed)* I don't...
MATHIAS. Yes, yes. Her French is beautiful. Go ahead.
ANNETTE. *(A beat, then—)* Bonjour. Como tallez vous?
BAPTISTE. Ah. Well. May I have my food now?
ANNETTE. Sure.

(Embarrassed now, she slams his drink on the table, and goes. After a moment, MATHIAS approaches.)

MATHIAS. I haven't seen you around these parts. What's your name?
BAPTISTE. My name is Baptiste Carbonneau.
MATHIAS. Pleased to meet you, Mr. Carbonneau. I don't know what Annie's so touchy about.
BAPTISTE. She is a woman.
MATHIAS. Oh, no no—she's well of course yes, she's a woman. She just a little rough around the edges sometimes, and you can't blame her. There's not a lot of people come through

here. So her manners can get a little raw, but she's a pure soul. I'm her father, you'll forgive me bragging a bit. So how is that stuff?

BAPTISTE. Fine, will you join me?

MATHIAS. Thanks, I think I will. *(MATHIAS pours himself a glass, refreshes BAPTISTE, then sets the bottle on the counter.)* So, you're from Canada. What are you looking for in these parts?

BAPTISTE. What is any man looking for?

MATHIAS. Only one answer to that in the Yukon.

BAPTISTE. Yes, well.

MATHIAS. You don't look like a prospector, though.

BAPTISTE. All the gold is gone, that is what I have been told.

MATHIAS. People look for it all the same. But you're right, you missed the action by nigh on twenty years.

BAPTISTE. You were here for the fever, then?

MATHIAS. We were here. And between you and me, I'm not sorry those days are behind us. Where are you from, Carbonneau?

BAPTISTE. I was raised in Montreal.

MATHIAS. Nice city?

BAPTISTE. Quite beautiful. Elegant, even.

MATHIAS. Educated?

BAPTISTE. The city is quite educated, yes.

MATHIAS. You, I meant.

BAPTISTE. Both the city of Montreal and myself have been educated.

MATHIAS. Well, you'ved come a long way. What brings you out here again? I didn't catch that.

BAPTISTE. I did not say.

MATHIAS. I know you didn't, that's why I'm trying to pry it out of you. No no. You don't want to say, I'm not going to push you.

BAPTISTE. And yet you ask me twice.

MATHIAS. *(Laughing)* Curiosity is a virtue! Didn't you ever hear that?

BAPTISTE. I have heard many things. Some of them are true. But not all.

MATHIAS. You're a philosopher.

BAPTISTE. Was that philosophical? I suppose it passes as such in Yukon.

MATHIAS. No no. You can't be cynical here. The weather won't stand for it. Fifty degrees below and the wind blowing at you straight out of the nether world, you learn pretty damn fast that cynicism is one of the luxuries of civilization.

BAPTISTE. Then you are a philosopher yourself.

MATHIAS. I am! Come a long winter's night, and out here the nights are long, you have time to ask yourself, what does it mean to be human, in the wilderness?

BAPTISTE. Some would say, to be human is to follow the laws of god. Just as the cosmos follows natural law, physical law, so must we follow the laws of the god in whose image we are made.

MATHIAS. Who would say that?

BAPTISTE. Some would say, it is known. Our reality is from God's decree, ordered, and this order represents the perfected nature of that god who has brought everything about, including the law itself.

(He laughs.)

MATHIAS. That's funny?
BAPTISTE. It is, a bit. The things we are taught, in our youth. And the things we learn elsewhere. Humanity is holy. Humanity is shit. So yes, I am educated, for all it is worth. You tell me yourself, in the Yukon, it is worth nothing at all.
MATHIAS. I didn't say that.
BAPTISTE. No? I thought you did.

(A beat.)

MATHIAS. So what are you doing here, Carbonneau?
BAPTISTE. I am having a glass of wine. Perhaps some food, if your pretty daughter deigns to feed me, and then I go to Minto Landing.
MATHIAS. That trail's under six feet of snow this time of year. What fool sent you there?
BAPTISTE. I am my own fool.

(ANNETTE enters, carrying two plates of food. She takes them to the table, sets them down, shy.)

ANNETTE. Here's your food. We had some chicken and carrots... *(Then, simple and sweet, schoolgirl French)* C'est un peu simple, mais j'espere que vous l'amez.
BAPTISTE. *(Surprised)* Merci bien, mademoiselle.
ANNETTE. De rien.

(She goes back to the bar, pleased with herself.)

BAPTISTE. *(To ANNETTE)* It is very good.

ANNETTE. Thank you.

(She starts to shove things back into the cabinets.)

MATHIAS. Annie, go on and make up a room for Mr. Carbonneau.
BAPTISTE. No, excuse me, I cannot stay.
MATHIAS. As my guest. We let you walk out that door tonight, it'd be just this side of murder. Amount to the same thing. Annie.
ANNETTE. *(Embarrassed)* If he doesn't want to stay, Pa—
MATHIAS. Annie. Make up a room.
ANNETTE. He is right, Mr. Carbonneau, you won't see sun now till almost midday tomorrow. You'd need a strong reason to go out there and face all that dark.
BAPTISTE. Perhaps not, then. My reasons for staying seem strong as well.

(BAPTISTE brings his empty wine glass to the bar, reaches for the bottle. Abashed, ANNETTE takes the glass from him.)

ANNETTE. Here, let me get that for you.
BAPTISTE. What is this?

(He looks at the counter, picks up a small open box that rests there, as she pours the wine.)

ANNETTE. Oh, that's nothing. Someone gave that to me a long time ago. I forgot it was back there.
BAPTISTE. What is it?

ANNETTE. It's bells. A Chinaman gave them to me, when I was just a little girl.
BAPTISTE. A Chinaman? What happened to him?
MATHIAS. He went back to China.

(Lights shift.)

Scene 4
Xuifei

XUIFEI. There was a girl in my village. When you looked at her, she would return your gaze like a young animal. Her hair fell to her shoulders like water, and although she rarely laughed, her smile was quick. I loved this girl. I wished to marry her. But her family was poor. My love had gone to someone so poor she could never marry and eventually she was sold, by her parents, to a house of prostitution. My brother, knowing my pain, came to me with this news as a gift. See, he said, I will give you money and now you can have her whenever you please. And that is what I did. Night after night I went into the village, and paid for the right to have her. But even that brought me no rest, and I could no longer bear the sight of her face. And so I left my home. I left my home.

(It is night. MATHIAS is alone in the inn. He has clearly been drinking. ANNETTE enters the scene behind him, as does

XUIFEI.)

ANNETTE. I can't do it!
XUIFEI. Kuh-yi, kuh-yi.

(XUIFEI rubs the balls expertly. She goes to watch him.)

ANNETTE. Show me!

(He does. She laughs, delighted, as he holds her hands and shows her how to rub the balls together.)

XUIFEI. Hao, hun hao!
ANNETTE. Pa, look! I can do it, too!
MATHIAS. Get out of here!

(XUIFEI disappears. ANNETTE turns, looks at MATHIAS, surprised.)

ANNETTE. You all right?
MATHIAS. *(Beat)* I'm fine, I'm fine. I'm just doing some bills, you got me so worked up about the money this afternoon, thought I'd see what we had in the till.
ANNETTE. You want me to stay with you?
MATHIAS. No, no. You go to sleep. *(She starts to go. He calls to her.)* Annie?
ANNETTE. Yeah, Pa.
MATHIAS. This Canadian. You like him?
ANNETTE. Oh my god.
MATHIAS. He's educated. Good looking. French.

ANNETTE. Go to bed, Pa.

MATHIAS. Best looking guy I've seen around here in years—

ANNETTE. GO TO BED.

MATHIAS. In a minute. *(She goes. MATHIAS looks at bills that have been left by the cash register, or on the counter.)* Two, two fifty, four, six—six hundred, just last month—that's down a bit from October, but still enough to put two hundred in the bank, which brings the savings up to over thirty thousand... *(After a moment, the sound of the bells, far off, can be heard. He turns, then turns back to his counting. The sound continues to rise as he counts.)*

Thirty thousand dollars, that's nothing to sneeze at, coming from nothing, most everybody else run through it all overnight, but Annette is going to have—her children are going to have more than I ever did. That's what matters. That's what matters! *(He stands, abrupt, listening. The sound fades. He takes another long drink.)*

People showing up out of nowhere, talk about nonsense, it's just the night. Night's so long now. So damn long...

*(He goes to the counter, turns up the light, which gets brighter
    and brighter until it suddenly goes out.
Blackout.)*

Scene 5

(CHARLIE wandering in the windy night, with SALLY and JIM behind him. He is going on. They are drinking and shoving each other, behind him. At some point they simply collapse in a drunken stupor.)

CHARLIE. I saw a bird. Last night of my life I slept in a real hotel, this place was swank, people wearing silk clothes, chairs with cushions on 'em. That bird was smart, it could talk in six different languages, some seaman taught him all this shit, then died on him, bird got dumped in this hotel in the wilderness, no one knew much more than that. So I go up to it—and I say, Hey bird! I hear you can talk! What do you have to say for yourself? And the bird just stares at me. So finally I think what the hell, and I turn around, and the bird says, "Thank god he's leaving. Boring old shithead." Turns out he won't talk to nobody unless you're walking away from him. I finally got sick of it, went off and got drunk. Come back, it's three in the morning maybe, I'm climbing the steps to the porch of this place and I hear a woman singing, this song of such purity, it's like a breeze from a far country, moving through the night, a dream of a better time. I never heard anything like it, before or since. And I look through the window, and it's that damn bird. All alone. Singing—well later they told me it was from some opera, that damn bird could sing opera on top of everything else. So the bird finally finishes this—song— and I say to it through the window—Bird, if you can do that— you can sing like that—how come you're so perverse? And that bird looks me in the eye and says, "Cause you're all sons of bitches."

(He stops, takes a drink. After a moment, SALLY laughs, long and hard.)

SALLY. That bird said that?
CHARLIE. *(Laughing)* It did. "Sons of bitches."
SALLY. That is a smart bird.

(She collapses again. JIM sits up.)

JIM. Where are we?
CHARLIE. We're right about here, you know. There's a windbreak up another half mile, we'll camp there.
JIM. We're sleeping out here? It's cold.
CHARLIE. Dammit Jim, I told you, we're going out to work that old stake Stu Campbell told us on!
JIM. No, come on.
CHARLIE. What'd you think we were doing, you damn drunk?
JIM. You just said... I need a drink.

(He staggers over to CHARLIE, looks for a bottle. CHARLIE tosses the bottle.)

CHARLIE. We're working now. That stake is still going strong. Stu used to swear on it.
JIM. It's going so good, how come he ain't out there working it?
CHARLIE. What do you care why? Nothing left for any of

us in the town.

JIM. Mathias takes care of us.

CHARLIE. I don't want to be taken care of! Goddammit, I'm not ready to just drink away my last years. I want to do something. I want to feel yearning in my heart. I want to climb into some freezing hellhole and look for gold. Remember that feeling?

JIM. Yeah, I remember it. That's why I drink, to forget it.

SALLY. *(Sitting up)* I'm not working any fool ass claim. There's no more gold out there, you fool.

CHARLIE. 'Cording to Stu Campbell there is. He said he and that Chinaman took near six thousand dollars out of the ground up there.

SALLY. That was a long time ago!

JIM. That where we're going?

CHARLIE. I told you this, Jim!

JIM. 'Cause I'm not going there.

SALLY. Jesus God above.

(She looks beyond them. MATHIAS stands in the snow, covered in blood. They turn and see what she sees. MATHIAS takes a step forward and tries to speak to them. After a moment, he collapses. They go to him, pick him up and help him stagger off.)

CHARLIE. Mathias!
SALLY. Oh my god, Mathias! What happened to him?
JIM. Mathias!
CHARLIE. Mathias!
SALLY. Look at all the blood, what happened?
JIM. Can he walk?

CHARLIE. Mathias, can you walk?
SALLY. What's he doing all the way out here? Mathias, what are you doing out here?
CHARLIE. You got him? You got him?

(In dark, ANNETTE rushes through the night.)

ANNETTE. Bring him upstairs, upstairs Mr. Carbonneau! Where did you find him? Oh my god, there's so much blood—somebody make coffee—blankets, I need blankets!

Scene 6

(BAPTISTE alone in the bar. He peers through the curtain into the back of the house, sees there is no one about, and starts to search the bar area. He pours himself a drink as he searches, then ducks back behind the bar itself, looking. ANNETTE comes out of the house, sees him behind the bar. He does not see her. After a moment, she speaks.)

ANNETTE. Can I help you?

(BAPTISTE stands, startled.)

BAPTISTE. No, no, I...ah, no.

(He goes to the other side of the bar. ANNETTE looks back at where he was looking, then looks up at him.)

ANNETTE. Looks like supplies are getting a bit thin back here.

(She pours him a drink.)

BAPTISTE. The prospectors who found your father on the trail, they came here once or twice, you were occupied, caring for him—
ANNETTE. So basically you just let them raid the place for a day and a half.
BAPTISTE. *(A shrug)* How is he?
ANNETTE. He'll be all right. I guess. I don't know. I haven't thanked you for what you did, Mr. Carbonneau.

(She brings him the drink she poured. He looks at her.)

BAPTISTE. I expected no thanks.
ANNETTE. You carry a man half a mile in the snow, and you don't expect thanks?
BAPTISTE. Expectations are wearisome.
ANNETTE. So are you.

(She turns, upset.)

BAPTISTE. Why are you so angry?
ANNETTE. I'm not angry. I'm grateful. I'm grateful! And I just thought I'd mention that, that I'm grateful that you saved my

father's life, 'cause I thought it might be something that was worth saying, thank you, thank you for saving my father's life. *(She pours herself a stiff drink, lifts the glass to toast him.)* So, thank you!

(He stops her hand. She looks at him.)

BAPTISTE. You're welcome. *(He takes the drink from her and drinks it himself.)* You must not drink. It will not help you. *(Beat)* You are worried for him. Yes? You are worried. For your father.

ANNETTE. I just don't understand what happened. He's been running on about the axe, and it's gone from the woodpile, but I can't make sense of any of it.

BAPTISTE. That is what he used to cut himself?

ANNETTE. It must be, but he says he doesn't remember. I don't know.

BAPTISTE. What was he doing so far out?

ANNETTE. He says he doesn't remember. *(Beat, tearing up)* I don't know what would happen to me, if anything happened to him. Sorry. I'm just scared. *(Wiping her eyes)* Do you have family, Mr. Carbonneau?

BAPTISTE. *(Surprised)* I? What makes you ask?

ANNETTE. I just can't make out why you'd be here. If you did. Why you'd leave them. The world is so lonely, even with there being just one person, that you love. At least my pa and I... we have each other.

BAPTISTE. You have your father? And that makes it not lonely?

(She shrugs.)

ANNETTE. No, it's still lonely. I don't know what I mean. It's this place, maybe. I don't know.

BAPTISTE. You think it is not so lonely elsewhere?

ANNETTE. I don't know what it's like, anywhere else, I only ever been here. And everything is so big and...distant, here. The mountains and the snow and the black nights can be so black.

BAPTISTE. And you feel alone.

ANNETTE. It is that, but not only that. There's the cold, too, sometimes it's so bitter it reaches right down to the heart of you, and you're thinking you must be a strong person, to bear something so otherworldly, and then the wind comes and you know you can't bear it, you're not strong, you're just like a ghost already, it takes the breath right out of you, just like that. Like death, that's how it feels. So you're going along and feeling that, and wondering how god could make a place so horrible, and you don't know if there is a god, you don't know if there's anything except the cold and the black and the wind, and then the lights come, blue and green and shimmering, all over the night sky. They just come, all at once. You see the stars again. And the mountains are so beautiful, the air is so strong, and you realize this terrible place is where god put his hand, back at the dawn of time. He just reached down and touched the earth, right here, that's why it's so strong. And then you're not lonely at all. *(Beat)* But you don't have anyone to tell that to. Which makes it a little lonely, I guess.

(A short beat, then—)

BAPTISTE. My father was a schoolteacher. He was well taught, by the Jesuits; at night he would play badly on the violin, he would quote endlessly from poets whose names are now lost. He was a good man who died needlessly when I was fourteen. My mother married again, a man who drank and beat her children. My sister, one night, he struck her so cruelly. Her face, her body. She was very young. He was a large man, I could not stop him. After her death, I would not stay.

(He pours himself another drink.)

    ANNETTE. I'm so sorry.
    BAPTISTE. I have seen worse since.

(As he is about to down another drink, she reaches out and places her hand on his, in a small gesture of comfort. He looks up at her, startled. They consider each other. After a moment, SALLY and JIM and CHARLIE enter.)

    CHARLIE. How is he?
    ANNETTE. He's fine. Just took a couple of nasty cuts, on his arm. That's how come all the blood. He's been unconscious, mostly. I won't say I wasn't real worried there for a minute, but he's come out of it now. *(Then)* I know you all been helping yourself around here.
    SALLY, CHARLIE, and JIM. No, no, no—
    ANNETTE. No, I was going to say, it's fine. I'm real thankful for your help. Jim Lynch, you take a seat. Sally, let me get you something. What can I get you?
    MATHIAS. *(Offstage)* Annie?

(ANNETTE turns, startled, as MATHIAS appears in the interior

doorway.)

ANNETTE. Pa, what are you doing up? You have to stay in bed.
MATHIAS. I'm all right.
ANNETTE. You're not all right.
MATHIAS. *(Sees BAPTISTE, bewildered)* What's he doing here?
ANNETTE. You asked him to stay. He was here, sleeping here, when Sally came and said they found you. On the trail.
SALLY. We found you out on the trail, Mathias, don't you remember? Couldn't carry you back the whole way. So Mr. Carbonneau, he come out and brought you in.
ANNETTE. He saved your life, Pa. Don't you remember any of this?
MATHIAS. Course I do. I'm just tired, is all. Little out of my head, I guess. Sorry.
BAPTISTE. How is your arm?
MATHIAS. Fine. Thanks for your help. Like a drink? Let me get you a drink. Jim, Charlie. She taking care of you? Let me take care of you.

(He goes to the bar, pours drinks.)

ANNETTE. Pa—
MATHIAS. How long I been sleeping?
ANNETTE. A day and a half.
MATHIAS. Guess I was tired. Charlie, Sally—how you holding up for food? You want some eggs, or something?
CHARLIE. I won't say no to a plate of eggs.

MATHIAS. She hasn't fed you yet? Annie, where are your manners?

ANNETTE. I've had a few things on my mind, Pa. And I don't think—

MATHIAS. What?

ANNETTE. I just don't want you to, to, to—Pa, really, you have to—

MATHIAS. I'm all right! *(He hands a glass of wine to BAPTISTE, pours himself a glass.)* I'm embarrassed, mostly. Go out to chop some wood for the stove and end up slicing up my own arm, the drunks from the town finding me wandering around the snow like some crazy prospector been lost in the hills since the fever hit.

BAPTISTE. You were a long way out.

MATHIAS. All that white, it's near impossible to find yourself once you're off the landmarks. Wind kicks up, there's no real way of knowing where you are. Isn't that right, Jim?

JIM. That's what I been saying, to Charlie, there ain't none of us in any shape to go out there no more. He's got some crazy idea.

CHARLIE. There's gold out there. Stu Campbell—

MATHIAS. Not tonight, Charlie. Let's just be grateful we're all safe and warm tonight. Annie, what about those eggs?

ANNETTE. *(To BAPTISTE)* Don't let him drink too much.

(She takes a moment, then goes. BAPTISTE watches. MATHIAS watches him.)

BAPTISTE. *(Off the others)* She did care for them. While you were sleeping. You've taught her well; she has a generous

heart.
MATHIAS. Thank you.
BAPTISTE. Can I ask you about these?

(He holds out the bells. MATHIAS stares at them for a moment, reaches for them, and takes them from BAPTISTE, firm.)

MATHIAS. Those things are still lying around, huh? Annie's gonna end up losing them, she's not careful.

(He takes the bells, starts to put them back in their box.)

BAPTISTE. She says it was a Chinaman who gave them to her. A prospector, Stu Campbell, he told me about this Chinaman as well. They worked a stake together, not far from here.
MATHIAS. *(Slight pause)* You've met Stu Campbell.
BAPTISTE. He said he was a good man. His name was Lin Xuifei. They were friends, it seems, and Campbell thinks something terrible must have happened to him; they had agreed to meet at Minto Landing, and the Chinaman never came.
MATHIAS. And why do you care about that?
BAPTISTE. I was paid to find him.

(A beat)

MATHIAS. You're a bounty hunter, then.
BAPTISTE. Yes. I am a bounty hunter.
JIM. *(Perplexed)* Someone put a bounty on the Chinaman? What for? He's been dead—

(BAPTISTE turns and looks at him. JIM looks at him.)

BAPTISTE. Why do you say that?
JIM. You're the one who said it. You said, Stu thinks something terrible happened to him. I don't know what happened to him.
MATHIAS. I don't know what any of us can tell you. It was a long time ago. None of us knew the man.
BAPTISTE. But he gave your daughter these bells.

(XUIFEI appears, holding bells out.)

XUIFEI. Shr-ni-da. Na ba. Na ba.

(ANNETTE enters, takes a step toward him, tentative.)

ANNETTE. What's he saying, Pa?
XUIFEI. Na ba! Na ba!

(MATHIAS casually takes up the other set of bells.)

MATHIAS. That's right, he came through, he gave those things to Annie, and then he left. Never got them to make that sound again and lord knows we tried. Charlie, you remember, how long were we trying to get these things to make that sound for her?
CHARLIE. Oh lord, it was months.
ANNETTE. Show me!
XUIFEI. Hao—

(XUIFEI holds her hands and shows her how to make the bells

ring.)

MATHIAS. Annie was heartbroken, everybody in town trying to get these damn bells to sing, nobody can do it. Sally—
SALLY. *(Cool)* I couldn't do it.
JIM. Just didn't have the touch, not a one of us. She was such a sweet little thing, you hated to disappoint her.
ANNETTE. You try it, Pa!

(She holds her set of bells out to him. He does not turn.)

MATHIAS. I still can't do it. Here, you give it a try.

(He hands his set of bells to BAPTISTE, who looks at them, considers them, then sets them down.
ANNETTE turns back to XUIFEI, hands him the bells. He shakes his head, and gives them back to her.)

XUIFEI. Jeige. Wo geh ni. Wo geh ni.
BAPTISTE. Stu Campbell, this prospector—
MATHIAS. A prospector! You're taking the word of a prospector, each and every one of them bone mad with gold fever to begin with—no offense, Charlie—
CHARLIE. None taken—
MATHIAS. By the time they make it through the Chilkoot Pass or whatnot, their brains and their hearts and their souls are frozen solid and blasted through, not a one of them even resembles a human being by the time they make it up here, that's who's telling you, what'd he say?
BAPTISTE. He said the Chinaman was carrying three thou-

sand dollars in gold. Do you remember that?

(XUIFEI empties a bag of gold onto his table.)

    ANNETTE. Pa, look!

(XUIFEI laughs, and gestures her to see it.)

    XUIFEI. Ni kan ba. Pyaon lian, shr bu shr?
    JIM. That what you're looking for? You talked to Stu, you're thinking that Chinaman froze out there, the gold's still out there?

(XUIFEI holds a piece up, shows ANNETTE.)

    XUIFEI. Wo gei ni.
    JIM. That gold is gone!
    BAPTISTE. You know that for a fact?
    JIM. Everybody knows it! How long ago was that, Sally?
    SALLY. Eighteen years.
    JIM. That's what I mean!
    CHARLIE. There's gold out there still! Stu told me, they never came to the bottom of that claim. We're gonna work it, me Sally and Jim.
    SALLY. Have a drink, Charlie.
    MATHIAS. Gold everywhere. Where is your god in so much gold, Carbonneau?
    BAPTISTE. My god? I have no relations with God. Do you?
    MATHIAS. I fear the Lord. But I question him, too. What I saw those years. Men driven mad with the wanting and the having and the losing of it. Standing in the icy waters day in day out,

the one becomes rich, the next dies of grief and loss, starvation, how many of us, dying of cold and starvation, scurvy. You ever see anyone die of scurvy? The blood turns thin. Legs go lame. Your gums swell and bleed until your teeth drop out, your skin mottles and putrefies—worthy men and women turning into lepers around us, my wife, my wife dying an unimaginable death, meanwhile God is showering gold without end on men living like animals. What kind of god is that? *(BAPTISTE does not answer. The two men look at each other, consider each other. XUIFEI stands and slowly leaves the room. ANNETTE takes her bells and leaves as well.)*

As to this Chinaman and his gold—I couldn't likely say one way or the other, what happened.

BAPTISTE. What year was this? Ninety-nine, ninety-eight?
MATHIAS. Ninety-nine.
BAPTISTE. Was that the year your wife died?

(MATHIAS looks at him, pours another drink.)

MATHIAS. Yeah, so I had other things to think about.
BAPTISTE. How big was the town at that time, do you remember?
MATHIAS. Lot of people coming through, those years.
BAPTISTE. But those who stayed, those who lived here. How many, thirty, forty?
MATHIAS. That sounds about right.
BAPTISTE. It was a hard winter.
MATHIAS. Yeah, it was.
BAPTISTE. People were starving, you said.
MATHIAS. Yes.

BAPTISTE. How did you make it through?

MATHIAS. You just do! I'm sorry. I don't mean to be so abrupt. It was a hard time. Hard to look back at it. We weren't here long ourselves, just arrived the year before, none of it looking like anything you thought. How could it? People tell you stories of gold without end, they don't tell you the rest, somehow. Met one guy, talked about the Yukon, he called it Eldorado. You hear that, you don't think about ragged men, living in shacks, held against the Northern wind with newspaper and glue. You don't think about the cold, going so deep for so long the memory of warmth moves to a distant place, it becomes the fantasy, a little girl's bedtime story. There once was a place where the sun shone, and things grew. You don't think, how can a woman and a child live in a place like that?

BAPTISTE. Your conscience bothers you, with regard to what you did?

MATHIAS. My conscience?

(A beat)

BAPTISTE. Bringing them, your wife and child, to this dreadful place.

(A beat)

MATHIAS. We were poor enough before we came here. I got no way of knowing what my life would've been if we never came. Just as you won't ever know what your life may've been, if you'd lingered on in the elegant city of Montreal, pondering the history of civilization.

(ANNETTE enters, carrying a bowl of eggs and sausages, for JIM and SALLY and CHARLIE.)

ANNETTE. Here you go! It's not much, I did what I could with what was in the kitchen—Pa. What's the matter?
MATHIAS. What?

(ANNETTE sets the food down, worried.)

ANNETTE. Look at you, you're all flushed, you look about to faint—
MATHIAS. I'm fine—
ANNETTE. You're not fine! *(Sharp to BAPTISTE)* I told you not to let him drink, it's making him sick. You shouldn't be drinking that stuff, it's been around I don't know how long, it's making you crazy, Pa.
MATHIAS. Guess I'm not used to it.
ANNETTE. Guess not. You're going back to bed right now.

(ANNETTE takes MATHIAS out. BAPTISTE turns to the others.)

CHARLIE. I'm sorry we can't help you, son. But no one here really knew that Chinaman. What'd you say his name was?
BAPTISTE. Xuifei. It means "snow."
CHARLIE. Well, that's an interesting fact, but you're missing my point here. We didn't even know his name. We all heard him and Stu were having some good fortune up there on that claim they struck, but he didn't come down here into town but a few times. Kept to himself, mostly. Didn't even speak English. There's not much more to say.

BAPTISTE. There is a good deal more to say, I think. Thank you for your help.

(BAPTISTE puts his rucksack on his shoulder and goes. There is silence for a moment. CHARLIE eats.)

SALLY. We got to get out of here.
JIM. That guy's an idiot. He's not gonna find him.
SALLY. He's no idiot.
JIM. You just like him, 'cause he's French.
CHARLIE. What do you want to stick around here for, Jim? I'm telling you, that claim is still out there and that cabin is snug. On top of, Stu left his traps! Catch us a few jackrabbits, steal a couple bottles of hootch from Mathias, we got everything we need.
JIM. *(Abrupt)* 'Member that Chinaman, how much gold he had? You and me working day and night, we didn't come up with four dollars between us. And he comes in here, a Chinaman, he don't even speak English, and the gold just come out of the earth for him. Rising up, out of the earth, like a bad dream.

(The lights shift.)

Scene 7
Xuifei

XUIFEI. My grief made me alone in the world. The desolation of the sea, the exhaustion which came with the loading and unloading of the vessels, the ebb and flow of tide, men, seasons, such days suited my bewildered spirit. But the nights of drinking and laughter were a torment to me. The women came at night and my heart filled with rage at the carelessness of empty pleasure. Even here, among a breed of men who were homeless in all the world, even here I could not stay. A ship came, sailing as far as anyone had heard. To a land of monumental mountains. Endless darkness. Cold beyond dreaming. Why would anyone go to such a place?

Scene 8

(JIM starts to sing. As the song progresses, the others join in.)

JIM.
Hark the herald angels sinngg.
Glory to, the newborn king.
Peace on earth, and mercy mild.
God and sinnnners reconciled.
Joyful all ye nations rise,

Join the triumph of the skiiiies,
With angelic host proclaim,
Christ is born in Bethlehem!
Hark the Herald Angels sing,
Glory to the newborn king.

(It is Christmas day. At the end of the song, there is a burst of applause from CHARLIE, SALLY, ANNETTE and MATHIAS.)

ANNETTE. That was beautiful, Jim.
JIM. Thank you.
MATHIAS. And it calls for another round. Annie!
ANNETTE. Pa—
MATHIAS. It's Christmas day, Annie. On Christmas day, one may be forgiven some small indulgence. The winter goes on a long time 'round here.
CHARLIE. That's the truth.
MATHIAS. Come on now, make everyone feel welcome, and I'll give you your present.
ANNETTE. A present!
MATHIAS. And what else, on Christmas?

(He reaches under the tree and picks up a box. He turns and hands it to her.)

ANNETTE. What is it?
MATHIAS. Open the box.

(She opens the box and takes out a beautiful hat, with gold and

stars on it.)

ANNETTE. Oh, how pretty! And it's for me?
MATHIAS. For whom else could it be? Not for Charlie!

(The others laugh as she puts the hat on, looking at herself in the mirror.)

ANNETTE. Oh, it's...I never saw anything so pretty...
SALLY. *(Dry)* I wonder what that Canadian will say?
JIM. He'll say she's the prettiest girl in the territory.
ANNETTE. Stop it! You're nothing but a bunch of lying, drunken—fools.
MATHIAS. No, they're not. They're telling you the truth. And you're a young lady now, you can just learn to accept a compliment. I didn't think it was possible anything could grow in this wild place, but it's like the whole land, the mountains and the air, just move through you and suddenly there's a spirit, right before you, where a child was a moment ago.

(A beat)

ANNETTE. Thank you, Pa.

(She hugs him.)

MATHIAS. It's my wedding present, Annie. The day of your marriage, I want you to wear it, and preserve it forever. You hear me? In twenty years, you promise me, you'll remember it was me who gave it to you?

ANNETTE. Now you're talking crazy.
MATHIAS. I don't think I am. Come on, everybody, drink, what the hell is the matter with you? Charlie, it's Christmas day and after I get you good and drunk you're going to tell us all that story about that dogsled race on Upper Bonanza.

(He pours more drinks.)

CHARLIE. That's a good story.
JIM. I heard that story so many times I think I'm gonna kill myself, I have to listen to it again.
MATHIAS. All right, not the dogsled story. What story we gonna get him to tell? Annie, what story you want to hear?
ANNETTE. Oh, I like all Charlie's stories.
MATHIAS. Well, pick one.
ANNETTE. I don't know.

(She goes to the tree, pulling out presents.)

SALLY. *(Dry)* So where'd that Canadian go, anyway?
ANNETTE. He disappeared two days ago, no one's seen hide nor hair of him since. Good riddance, I say.
JIM. He's still off looking for that Chinaman?

(The sound of bells. MATHIAS turns, distracted, tries to focus. This is bad news.)

ANNETTE. He didn't say one way or the other, he just went. Coming here and stirring up a lot of trouble over nothing. Here, Pa, there's still presents. You open yours.

(She hands him a present.)

    MATHIAS. It's not enough.
    ANNETTE. What do you mean? *(Beat)* Pa? Aren't you going to open it? *(The sound of the bells continues to grow.)* Pa?
    MATHIAS. I don't need any gifts, I tell you. It's not enough.
    ANNETTE. You give so much to everyone. It's just a little thing. Look, it's a scarf. I made it myself.

(She shows it to him. He looks at her, suddenly hugs her.)

    MATHIAS. Annie.
    JIM. Mathias, you all right?
    ANNETTE. He's okay, of course he's okay. It's okay, Pa. You're just drinking too much these days.

(MATHIAS tears the scarf off his head.)

    MATHIAS. I'm fine, I'm fine—

(He reaches for the bottle.)

    ANNETTE. Oh, Pa—
    MATHIAS. I'm fine, I said! It's Christmas, I can have a drink, can't I? *(He drinks from the bottle. ANNETTE looks down.)* I'm sorry. I'm sorry, Annie, you're right, I guess I am a little— god, what the hell is— *(Frantic now)*
    What the hell you all staring at? It's Christmas, the day of our lord's birth, how come you're not—we should bow our heads to the lord, in prayer. That's what we need to do, now. Every-

body, now, join me— *(He kneels. The others do too. The sound of the bells continue throughout.)*

Oh, Lord—Lord we thank you for our life's many blessings. You guide and protect us in the wilderness, and bring us out of our—out of our grief and despair, your strong right hand protects us oh god—god, don't you hear it? Doesn't anyone hear it?

(He stands, sudden. The bar fades in darkness. The walls fall apart, revealing XUIFEI, in the distance, in the snow.)

End of Act I

ACT II

Scene 9

(There is a campfire. Directly alongside, MATHIAS sits alone at the bar. The walls are gone. XUIFEI stands alone, speaks.)

XUIFEI. The way is a limitless vessel. Used by the self, it is not filled by the world. Such is what I was taught. I could not be of the world. And yet the world overwhelmed me. Nature is not kind, it treats all things impartially. Neither is man kind. In the wilderness of nature, we learn who we are.

(MATHIAS looks over at him, then looks away.)

MATHIAS. You don't have to think about that. *(He goes to the bar, pours himself a glass of wine. As he speaks XUIFEI disappears.)* That was a long time ago. You carried it long enough, it don't have to mean everything. A life is more than one moment, one day, that's not a life. Every good you do isn't erased by one necessity, that's what it was, a single necessity, no one said they wanted it. I didn't want it. Last moment I ever felt truly alive, all the hammering, pushing it away, you think a man wants that to be what is? I didn't ask for this. It had to happen, someone had to do it, it fell to me. Last moment I ever felt alive. Who would choose that? But somebody had to. Both of us a sacrifice.

For all the rest. *(In shadow, a figure stands at the open door.)*
Not just Annette, but all of them, how many lives was that winter meant to take? She was starving, every last one of us looking death in the eye. Somebody had to do something.

JIM. Mathias?

(The figure steps into the light. It's JIM.)

MATHIAS. *(Turning, startled)* Jim Lynch! Come on in, what are you doing out there on a night like this?

JIM. Who you talking to?

MATHIAS. Just myself. What can I get you, a cup of whiskey?

JIM. Well, I wouldn't say no to that. Never could, you know that. *(MATHIAS pours him a drink.)* I heard you talking in here, thought maybe that Canadian came back, or something. Thought that maybe was who you were talking to.

MATHIAS. No, haven't seen him.

JIM. How long's it been now?

MATHIAS. Don't know, three days maybe.

JIM. Damn cold out there, too. Maybe he froze or something.

MATHIAS. Maybe.

JIM. Anyway, that's who I thought you was talking to. He's a talker, that one, isn't he?

MATHIAS. You been talking to him, Jim?

JIM. No, now you know I wouldn't do that. I was just thinking about the other night. Before he took off. You two were kind of going at it. He had a lot of questions. He's a persistent guy.

MATHIAS. *(Acknowledging the truth of this)* He'd've been

a prospector, I'd lay odds on his chances, hitting something eventually.
JIM. I was thinking that myself.
MATHIAS. You need another drink?

(He pours them both another round.)

JIM. Can't pay you for it. I'm plumb broke, Mathias, and that's a fact.
MATHIAS. Don't worry about it. Your money's no good here.
JIM. I don't have any money.
MATHIAS. That's fine, Jim.

(JIM downs the second drink.)

JIM. Of course, regarding this matter I don't think he's gonna be able to find nothin'. After all this time? You got to ask yourself, if there was anything out there anymore, somebody would've found it by now. Every inch of this land been racked and raped clean, Alaska ain't so big we couldn't suck dry every inch of it, all that gold in the ground. This place sure is cozy! You built it up nice, over the years. Got your own little kingdom up here. Be a shame if anything happened to take that away, considering what you had to do to get it. *(Beat)* I'd like another drink, Mathias.

(MATHIAS considers this, now, then pours the drink.)

MATHIAS. You been mentioning these thoughts to anyone,

Jim? Sally, or Charlie, maybe?

JIM. No, no.

MATHIAS. It's just I haven't seen much of them, since the Christmas party.

JIM. They're scared, Mathias.

MATHIAS. What are they scared of?

JIM. That's what I said! But Charlie, he's all, gonna go work that stake again, up by Fortymile. The one Stu Campbell and that Chinaman worked. He wants gold. I understand that. I just don't want to go back out into the wilderness to get it.

(A beat)

MATHIAS. Don't I take care of you, Jim?

JIM. Maybe I don't want to be taken care of no more. You ever think about that? Feels good to be the king, don't it, always doling out favors. Never crosses your mind, maybe a man would want more than that.

MATHIAS. Don't do this, Jim. What happened was a necessity. Good for all of us then and now. A man can't be held responsible for something that had to happen anyway. Let it rest. I'm begging you. Let it rest.

(The two men consider each other.)

JIM. *(Not unkind)* It's not in my interest, Mathias. You ever think about that? Course you didn't. You never had to, till now.

MATHIAS. You gonna make me go back there, Jim? I kept it at bay all this time and now you're going to make me go back?

JIM. Don't talk to me, talk to that Canadian. All these years, no one ever wanted to know. But he wants to know now. So whyn't you open the till there, see how much you got on hand. Then we'll talk about what's in the bank.

(MATHIAS nods, brief, backs away.)

    MATHIAS. That's Annie's money. Money for her children. Yours I put elsewhere.
    JIM. What do you mean?
    MATHIAS. All of a sudden you're rich? Where'd you get the money from, so suddenly? That Canadian makes it back here, you're the one he's gonna be looking at. You and me both.
    JIM. We'll tell him I hit a stake.
    MATHIAS. That's exactly right. That's it, Jim. That's why I prepared for this. Knowing this day was coming. Your share is out there. We just got to go get it.

(The bar starts to shift, as JIM considers the wilderness.)

    JIM. What do you mean, we got to get it?
    MATHIAS. Where does gold come from, Jim? Ask yourself. Where does it come from?

Scene 10

(Lights shift. The wilderness. XUIFEI, in the snow.)

XUIFEI. The gold came out of the earth for me. I did not ask it to. I was so lost in my own mind, this wild place seemed to suit me, for a time, and I was uncomplaining. Silence was my way. Grief and private bitterness were my way, until the gold came. And then I saw envy in the faces of all who looked on me. The hunger of men half dead with exhaustion, hunger not for food or warmth or wisdom or peace, but hunger for these lumps of stone which I held so carelessly in my hand. These stones held meanings for them which I could not comprehend. This was not my heart's desire. The truth of this overwhelmed me, and I knew, I must go home. I must take this strange fortune, given to me by the earth itself, and buy the girl I loved and defiled, buy her and bring her to my home, and make my life with her. That was my intent.

(Behind him, a body stirs, moves.)

BAPTISTE. *(Hoarse)* Is someone there? Who is there? Help me, please. *(BAPTISTE tries to sit up and look around, lost, blinded by the snow and the dark. He babbles for a long moment in French, then, delirious, reaches into his pack and takes out a gun. He swings it around, points it at XUIFEI. XUIFEI looks at him. BAPTISTE stares.)* It cannot be.
XUIFEI. A weapon will not help you here.
BAPTISTE. The Chinaman. You are the Chinaman.

XUIFEI. This place will take you. The darkness without end. The cold there is no name for. This is death, I tell you. I know it now as I know myself.

(He starts to go. BAPTISTE crawls after him.)

BAPTISTE. Help me. Help me, please. I am lost. Help me find my way. I will freeze, here, I will die, please—

(XUIFEI turns on him, angry.)

XUIFEI. Pain and disappointment are meant to cleanse the heart. Yours have lead you astray! There is no place on earth that offers rest for such as you. There is no place for any of us. I cannot help you now.
BAPTISTE. I am here for you. I came for you.
XUIFEI. You came for desolation! You came for the hope that your empty spirit might be filled by a place so wild and cold and evil that God himself cannot utter a curse to contain it. You came as I did, in love with your own self-pity. You are beyond help.

(But as he tries to turn again, BAPTISTE grabs him and wrestles him to the ground. The two men fight again, until BAPTISTE falls backward, into the snow. XUIFEI stands.)

BAPTISTE. I would live. I would not die here. It is so cold. I would die, where the warmth of the sun might find me one last day. Where the heart might leap with joy at the sight of a woman's face. I would see a woman gaze upon me with kindness, one last time. Can you have no compassion?

(XUIFEI looks at him, mournful. After a moment, he speaks.)

    XUIFEI. It is a poor thing, from this side of the grave, but I would have justice.
    BAPTISTE. I will bring you justice. Please. Let me live.
    XUIFEI. He who regards himself as the world may accept the world. I would not have you die here. It is too lonely.

(XUIFEI points in the opposite direction. BAPTISTE turns, sees light.)

    BAPTISTE. *(Hoarse)* C'est une lumiere. Je le vois. Le lumiere.

(XUIFEI goes in the direction of the light. BAPTISTE follows, first crawling, then standing and staggering off.)

Scene 11

(In the snow, MATHIAS appears, with JIM. MATHIAS carries an axe, and a pack. JIM carries a bottle.)

    JIM. It can't be this far. You didn't say it was this far.
    MATHIAS. We're there now. We're here, it's right here.

(A flash. XUIFEI is watching them.)

JIM. God, it's just like it was. You buried it? Goddammit, Mathias, you buried it?

(MATHIAS reaches into his pack, hands JIM another bottle.)

MATHIAS. We'll take turns.
JIM. Digging in the ground for gold. I told Charlie I never would come back here.

(A flash, CHARLIE in the distance.)

CHARLIE. There's gold out there, Jim. Only thing that's gonna save any of us.
JIM. Where is he? You hear that? Charlie?
MATHIAS. No one there, Jim. Have another drink, it'll warm you up.

(JIM drinks.)

JIM. *(Desperate)* Shouldn't be out here. You missed it, Mathias!
MATHIAS. I didn't, it's right here!
JIM. I don't see no markings! How can you tell anything, all this white. Nothing. It's just blank nothing.

(He drinks. A flash, SALLY appears.)

SALLY. We got to get out of here, Jim! You more than anybody!

JIM. Sally? Sally! Charlie!

MATHIAS. They're not here. We're the only ones here, Jim.

SALLY. I don't know what happened, and I don't want to know! I don't want to look at your palm no more, you don't have to show me nothin'!

JIM. It wasn't me, Sally. I didn't do it!

MATHIAS. Jim, your brain's half mad with that stuff.

JIM. You remember the horses? On the dead horse trail? Just moving through the night, dumb beasts beat so hard they was half mad with it, almost human with all that suffering. So many dying those years. What would it matter, one more? What does one more matter?

MATHIAS. Have another drink, Jim! You don't have to think about that now!

JIM. Why'd we ever come here, Mathias? Do you remember?

(A flash, XUIFEI appears, watching, and disappears again.)

MATHIAS. I remember the streets of Seattle. The word, that gold was here. The hope that come up in your chest, that there was a chance of life opening up in new ways, that somehow the size of this place would mean...

(A flash on ANNETTE, wearing her hat, in the snow, looking at the sky.)

JIM. Mean what?
MATHIAS. Everything.

THE BELLS

JIM. I didn't come for that. I came for gold. *(He grabs the pickaxe, drunk, tries to raise it to dig. Another flash on XUIFEI. JIM backs away, startled.)* Did you see him? He's out here! Mathias, the Chinaman is out here!
MATHIAS. Now you're talking crazy.
JIM. You take me back. How do I get back?
SALLY. Jim!
CHARLIE. Jim!
JIM. Charlie? Sally!
MATHIAS. It's the wind.
JIM. *(Starting to cry)* Take me home, Mathias. I want to go home.

(A flash, XUIFEI appears, watching.)

MATHIAS. Have another drink, my friend.

(He hands the bottle to JIM, who falls into the snow, sobbing.)

JIM. It's cold.

(JIM continues to sob. MATHIAS comforts him.)

MATHIAS. It's all right, Jim. It's time to just slow down, let everything slow down for you. Just go to sleep. Everything's fine. You've known a long time that this place would finally get you. Been here so long you're a part of it. I know I am. *(He stands, moves away, looks around him.)* Night, day. Wind. Stars. Seasons. It's a dance, isn't it, Jim? And our task, maybe—maybe our task is simply to find our place in it. Don't argue with it. Don't try to understand the whole of it. Just find your place, and move with it. What did the ancients say about movement? That Canadian would know. He's a smart one, he thinks he's going to trick me into admitting, what? What do you think he thinks I did? Why does he want to know? He made me angry, I admit it, and anger is the enemy. But I've had a lot of time to prepare for all of this. Obviously I couldn't just pretend it wasn't going to happen. I hoped, of course, one always hopes, but hope is the frailest of virtues. I don't know that it isn't a failing, finally. Hope. Ah, I'm wandering. I'm tired, Jim. I got to be honest, I was relieved when you came to me tonight. Not that I've been looking forward to this, far from it. But that I knew it would finally be over. Another necessity. A hard one, one I deeply regret, but I was worn down by the, what, the inevitability of it. Your coming, in the night. You were always going to come, alone, in the night. It was in your nature, my friend! Your part of the dance. And I was just the agent. I fought it, you can't deny that, I begged you not to bring us out here again, I've been fighting the whole of it all along, but some things will not be denied. I'm stating the obvious. This is boring, I'm boring you! But the fact is, if you hadn't come, it wouldn't have been fated, don't you see? It would have just been my imagination going haywire all these years, eating itself up with worry for no cause. That's all it would have been! Tracks in my mind, grooves where my thoughts wore down whatever it was used to be in there. Horror. Goodness. I'm still good. I did not, the proof being it meant something to me. It was a sacrifice. It's not the goodness that's gone, it's the horror, that's what I faced. Alone. All these years. You didn't have to face any of it. You just reaped the benefits. You and Charlie and Sally and all the rest, who knew! We all knew together, and you didn't want the knowledge, you couldn't face it, that's why you didn't see this coming. But I did. I did. Because I understand treasure. The idea of treasure, I saw it work on too many minds. I saw reason itself bend under the weight of it. Bend so far that the universe itself ceases to exist! The mind. So many things flashing like lightning through the mind. This world isn't so big we can't erase it altogether! With hunger. Fear. Greed. Memory. Not memory, the past doesn't exist if you don't let it. There's no such thing as memory! Tracks. But it's a battle. Because that's what happens, isn't it? When you spin. You work it all out. Again, and again and again, you catch yourself, two people, all the time, the one watching and planning and holding the rest at bay, I'm not looking at that, the not looking itself is exhausting, and so lonely, in the middle of so much accomplishment, to be so alone, you can't deny all of it was an accomplishment. Annie. The lives of, all life, what I did, and to never rest, you don't even know how lucky you are, this is an easy destiny, quiet, falling silent, sleep-drenched, into the snow. It's a kindness. Becoming a part of the world you threw away, and for what? Gold? Liquor? A kindness. I mean to be kind. No. I am not apologizing to anyone! Goddamned Chinaman can go to hell. There is no Chinaman. He's a track, in my mind. Eighteen years. Every second, a lifetime. I'm not looking at that. The world is so pretty. The stars are so pretty. Beautiful. Even in the dead of night, the snow shines, the mountains, black against black, all of it a wonder and it's always here. Look at it, Jim! And we can't hardly ever even see it, because there's too much going on in the mind. Look, Jim! The lights! The world is so beautiful, and so alone. It's lonely. It's lonely for us. I see that now. I see that. *(He turns and sees XUIFEI, watching.)*

You here. I knew you would be. *(Beat)* Look over him. Look over him.

(He heads off. XUIFEI watches him go.)

Scene 12

(SALLY and CHARLIE make their way through the snow.)

SALLY. We got to go in, Charlie. It's too cold.
CHARLIE. We got to find Jim!
SALLY. What did he come out here for anyway?
CHARLIE. I don't know, but we got to find him before we go back!
SALLY. I can't keep going! Charlie—

(She stops. XUIFEI is there. CHARLIE comes up behind her.)

CHARLIE. Good god.
SALLY. It's the Chinaman.
CHARLIE. You see him too?
SALLY. Please don't hurt us. We didn't know what happened. We just didn't ever really know.

(She falls to her knees. XUIFEI steps forward.)

CHARLIE. What do you want? What do you want, Ghost?

(XUIFEI holds out his hand to her, palm upward.)

SALLY. You want me to read your palm? I can't read your palm, Ghost.

(XUIFEI continues to hold out his palm.)

CHARLIE. Do it, Sally.
SALLY. That's just a trick, Charlie! I can't really do it under the best of circumstances!
CHARLIE. What is it you want us to know, Ghost?

(XUIFEI looks at them, looks at his palm.)

SALLY. What's he saying, Charlie?
CHARLIE. I don't hear nothing but the wind.

(XUIFEI looks at them, desolate. SALLY takes a step forward.)

SALLY. Look at him, he's crying. Don't cry, Ghost.
CHARLIE. Ghost, let me tell you a story, Ghost. About an old prospector, one day he wakes up, starts to make himself some coffee, turns around and there's another prospector, heading down the road, moving away from him, and the first one says come on over here, let me make you some coffee and biscuit! So the stranger comes on over, sits by the fire and the prospector looks at him and says, you know what friend, I think I know you. All my life, he said, I been out here searching for treasure. I have sought it in on mountaintops and in valleys of snow and ice. I have sought it in the wind and the cold, in the roiling waters fal-

ling to the sea, I have sought it deep in the earth itself—and yet have not found it. Instead, at the end of every trail, I have found you. Nothing else. No one else. And I cannot yet say who you are. Tell me, stranger. Who are you?

(A beat)

    SALLY. What did the stranger say?
    CHARLIE. He knows what he said.

(XUIFEI points to JIM's body.)

    SALLY. Jim? *(CHARLIE and SALLY hurry to the place where JIM's body has been revealed.)* Jim? Jim!
    CHARLIE. Aw, Jim.
    XUIFEI. You must bury him.
    SALLY. How can we bury him? The ground is frozen solid.
    XUIFEI. You must bury him, or he will never rest.

Scene 13

(ANNETTE, with a lamp, outside the bar.)

    ANNETTE. Is someone there? Who is there? Who is it? Who is it?

(A figure staggers forward and collapses on her.)

BAPTISTE. Je te supli—la lumiere—
ANNETTE. Mr. Carbonneau—
BAPTISTE. Annette—
ANNETTE. Oh my god—you've been out there this whole time—
BAPTISTE. I did not understand. To love death, that is a sin. But perhaps, to find meaning at the edge of death—
ANNETTE. Mr. Carbonneau—you stop now, stop—we got to get you inside—

(MATHIAS appears at the edge of the clearing. He watches and listens as she takes BAPTISTE inside.)

BAPTISTE. *(Overlap)* What I was told, as a child, the promise of meaning and justice, why is that taken from us, Annette?
ANNETTE. *(Overlap)* Mr. Carbonneau, you're froze, please let me help you, please— *(He suddenly kisses her. She resists, then kisses him back. MATHIAS sees this, unseen.)* It's all right now. You're gonna be all right. *(Sees MATHIAS, embarrassed)* Pa, there you are, where'd you go? Mr. Carbonneau came back, he's near froze—
BAPTISTE. I saw him. I tell you. I saw him.
MATHIAS. Baptiste. Son. Just let Annette take care of you now.
ANNETTE. I'm gonna take your boots off now. There's coffee in the kitchen, Pa—
MATHIAS. I'll get it. I'll get some blankets, too.

(He turns and goes into the next room.)

ANNETTE. *(Pulling off Carbonneau's boots)* You got to be still, let us help you now. *(Calling)* Pa, you got to heat up some water—
MATHIAS. *(Off)* I know, I know—
BAPTISTE. *(To ANNETTE)* I came here with a bitter heart, I came for money alone, but now I understand—
ANNETTE. Wandering in the wilderness for three days, it's crazy, everybody's gone crazy lately—I said be still, now—

(Just then, the sound of the wind. XUIFEI opens the door, comes into the room. He closes the door. BAPTISTE stands at the sound of it.)

BAPTISTE. Who is it? Who is there? Who is there?

(MATHIAS, reentering, sees XUIFEI. He looks at BAPTISTE, surprised, shrewd.)

MATHIAS. You see something? What do you see?
BAPTISTE. You see him too.
MATHIAS. Annette, go get that coffee. Go on.

(She goes.)

BAPTISTE. I found the signs of what has been. The blasted earth. Snow and ice, the signs of fire!
MATHIAS. *(Reasonable)* Prospectors burn the ground, so

they can bring out the gold. It's the only way, the ground's so frozen, the only way to get it out is to scorch the earth.

(BAPTISTE reaches into his knapsack and pulls something out. Still shivering, he puts it on the table. It is a blackened skull. ANNETTE returns with the coffee and sees this.)

BAPTISTE. I found him.
ANNETTE. What is that? Why do you bring that here?
BAPTISTE. Annette—
MATHIAS. Annette, go into the kitchen.
ANNETTE. *(Near tears)* Pa.
MATHIAS. *(With compassion)* Go on now, honey. Go heat some water, make up a bath. It'll be all right. Go on. *(ANNETTE goes. MATHIAS pours coffee.)* Drink this. You need it. *(BAPTISTE ignores this, he shrugs.)* You're not interested in this coffee, how about a glass of wine?
BAPTISTE. I will tell them what you did.
MATHIAS. What I did? And what do you think you know about that?
BAPTISTE. I know he was here. He came to this place, he had three thousand dollars. He disappeared in the night, and you became a wealthy man.
MATHIAS. I see. This is about greed. I can't say I'm surprised, I've seen my share of that over the years. How much are they paying you? I can match it. I can double it.
BAPTISTE. I will not take your blood money!
MATHIAS. You came here for blood money! You got a price, you already admitted that much. My guess is, right about now your price is going up. Maybe I'll pay it, and maybe I won't.

BAPTISTE. *(Insistent)* I will take this to the authorities. I will tell what I have seen, what I know. I will tell them the truths that you have been hiding—

MATHIAS. *(Laughing)* There are so many truths! I didn't think I'd have to remind you of that. One truth is, we were starving. We supposed to die that way, like animals? Go from one night into the next, you telling me that's what life is meant to be? Because I don't believe that. I believe in the power and the flexibility and the resourcefulness of the human spirit. You find yourself in a far country, you learn to adapt. You forget what you learned in a previous life. Because if you cling to what it is you thought you knew? You die. And that was not going to happen.

BAPTISTE. Then you admit it.

MATHIAS. I admit that we were living with death, among the dead. Dreams come to you in the cold. Odd moments, you waken from a stupor, see the one you're meant to care for, and you know, this can't go on, you have to do something to stop it or it will be too late. It's not merely your own survival. And in those few moments you know that, survival becomes a bigger thing. Becomes part of the place itself.

BAPTISTE. What did you do, Mathias? To survive.

(MATHIAS looks at him. After a beat, he answers.)

MATHIAS. I wrote. To my wife's folks, after she died. That's how it ended. They sent money, for the baby. Lot of money. Enough for everybody.

BAPTISTE. I can write too. I can find out. It is the easiest thing in the world, to find out.

MATHIAS. Drink your wine. Go take a bath.

(He picks up the skull by the sockets of the eyes, and carries it casually to the bar, pours them both drinks.)

BAPTISTE. This is not a matter of a casual argument to be won or lost. The act of taking a man's life is not something to be toyed with, it is not a game—
MATHIAS. You're the one who keeps changing the rules.
BAPTISTE. *(Incensed now)* I met the parents. They are good people. They have searched for their son for fifteen years. They carry their grief across oceans, through the insurmountable barriers of time and language and place so that they may find their son and bring him home, if, as they fear, he is dead, to bring him home so that he may be buried with his ancestors, in his home. With his people. His spirit cannot rest until he is brought home.
MATHIAS. Who told you that? God? Oh that's right, you and God don't get along. Reason then. "His spirit cannot rest"— maybe not reason. Superstition, then? Is that what we're arguing about now? Superstition?
BAPTISTE. It is an ancient belief. The Greeks themselves. The Egyptians. The necessity of a proper burial— It is a necessity—
MATHIAS. Life is full of necessities.
BAPTISTE. And death as well.
MATHIAS. *(Laughing)* Meaning what?
BAPTISTE. *(Defiant)* You ask me if it is my god or my reason that tells me the truth, and I tell you it is my heart. My heart tells me you killed him. You killed him, and I will see you brought to justice.

(A beat, and then, ANNETTE calls from the other room.)

ANNETTE. Pa?

(BAPTISTE turns, at the sound of her voice.)

MATHIAS. *(Lighting on this)* Is that all your heart tells you? *(Calling)* It's okay, honey, I'll be right there. *(Turning back)* What would you do for her? She was in danger, say, mortal danger, what would you do?
BAPTISTE. *(Deflecting)* No, no—
MATHIAS. Would you kill for her? Think now, before you answer. Think about the way she's entered your heart. It's just starting, but it would take a blind man not to see it. Both of you are running through each other's spirits, like a river finding new ways. I don't begrudge you, you want to take her from me, I see that, and I don't begrudge you. I'm not a monster. I recognize what that is. So tell me. Would you kill for her?
BAPTISTE. No I would not. I would not.
MATHIAS. Course not.
BAPTISTE. You do not know me.
MATHIAS. I know when you're lying.
BAPTISTE. And I know your lies as well.
MATHIAS. I know you do. I just don't think you're really finally going to be able to do anything about it. For all your hunting and truth seeking out there on the blasted earth—I'm her father. You'd lose her forever, I'd see to that. And for what? Money? Oh that's right, this isn't about money anymore. This is about justice. Meaning. A dead man. None of it real. All of it tracks in the mind.
BAPTISTE. No. I know this now. Conscience. We cannot live without conscience. Perhaps it is not only justice we must

seek. Perhaps it is redemption. If you only spoke the words. To no longer carry the burden alone. What about your soul, Mathias?

MATHIAS. My soul is steady. Yours, I think, is not. You went out there, to the edge of reason, and what did you see?

BAPTISTE. I saw Xuifei.

(There is another silence as the two men consider what this means.)

MATHIAS. You saw him. Alone, in the wilderness, you saw his spirit rising frozen from the grave. And you see him now, is that right? You're seeing ghosts, son. You keep pursuing this, that's what your life is going to be. Ghosts. Night. Desolation. Madness.

BAPTISTE. There's madness here.

MATHIAS. No. This is sanity I'm offering you now. Think about her. Tell me what you would do for her, if you loved her, if you came back to life just that far, what you know in your heart you'd be capable of doing, to protect her, and then think what if she were your child? You just take a minute and think about that. What having a child, protecting a child, what that might drive you to.

BAPTISTE. *(Quiet)* Even so. If it drove me to kill. Unjustly. I would expect to hang for it. We cannot survive as a people if we look the other way when a man's life has been taken so cruelly.

MATHIAS. Just because your heart's made room for a little light, doesn't mean the darkness fades.

BAPTISTE. You cannot excuse what you did! I cannot excuse it—

MATHIAS. Nothing happened! Look around! What you got here is a town with a nameless crime without a victim. This is your evidence that something happened? *(Off the skull)* The land is littered with them. It doesn't prove a thing. Men came here and died here and no one knows who they were, why they were, how they died, why they died. Why they lived. No one cares. Go ahead, take it up to the law at Fortymile, see for yourself. They'll laugh at you. They'll shrug. It doesn't mean anything.

BAPTISTE. I will tell her, then. If that is the only justice he can have, he will have it. I will tell her.

(MATHIAS freezes.)

MATHIAS. She won't believe you.

BAPTISTE. She knows it already. If the words were spoken, there would be no question inside of her. It would be known. Forever. By her. She would know you. As you are.

MATHIAS. I'll kill you. I'll—kill you. *(He takes him by the neck, and starts to strangle him. BAPTISTE puts up a fight, but MATHIAS has him.)* You'll die alone, and she'll die alone. Do you doubt it? Listen. Listen to what's out there. Silence. Doom. Madness. So, tell me. Do you want to live? Do you? *(He tosses him, sudden, to the floor. BAPTISTE chokes, gasping for breath. MATHIAS moves away.)*

This land's not going to claim either one of you. Even if survival means the betrayal of everything you believe in, you'll survive. I'm telling the truth, now. You're a man who recognizes truth. It's going to happen. It's happened already.

(ANNETTE reenters.)

ANNETTE. Pa—Baptiste—is he all right?

MATHIAS. He's just tired. *(She helps him up.)* You got something you want to say to Annie, Mr. Carbonneau?
BAPTISTE. *(Beat)* No.
MATHIAS. Then I think she's made up a bath for you. *(BAPTISTE lets ANNETTE take him off. MATHIAS turns to XUI-FEI.)* You need to go now. There's nothing for you here. He's staying here.

(XUIFEI leaves. Lights fade.)

Scene 14

(MATHIAS, in the bar, drinking alone, in the night. The skull is on the bar. ANNETTE enters.)

ANNETTE. I put him in your bed. He didn't want to go.
MATHIAS. He's half out of his head. I hope you insisted.
ANNETTE. I did, of course I did.
MATHIAS. Is he sleeping?
ANNETTE. Yes. Saying such godawful crazy things, Pa. I'm glad you weren't up there, to hear him.
MATHIAS. A week in the cold, digging for bones in the scorched earth. That must have been some ordeal. He'll get through it. You go up there. You spend the night at his side.

Don't listen to any of his crazy ramblings, he's out of his head, right now. When he wakes up, you just tell him you care for him. Hold onto his hands. Remind him who he is. He'll make it through.
    ANNETTE. *(Quiet)* What did you do, Pa?
    MATHIAS. I didn't do anything. *(Beat)* I didn't do anything. *(Beat)* I love you.

(ANNETTE backs away from him.)

    ANNETTE. Please don't. I can't. I'm sorry. I can't.

(Unable to look at him, she goes. After a moment he goes to the bar, pours himself more wine.)

    MATHIAS. What does it mean to be human in the wilderness? Might as soon ask what it means to be human anywhere, but that's not the question, is it. The question is here. What does it mean, in this crushing place. God knows it's not that I don't believe in the light of us, I know what it is when the darkness is all we have, we're not meant to live like that. If we were, death would mean nothing. Instead it looms. Like this place. And so we cling to the days, even as they disappear around us. Gather around the light of a fire. A Christmas tree, a young girl. A woman. We don't just give in to the night. We turn our faces to the sun. That's what it means. To be human. To live. Simply, to live. *(He picks up the skull, considers it.)* Not this. This doesn't look like anything at all. *(The sound of bells. MATHIAS freezes, shakes his head.)* I won't look any more. It's over.
    JIM. How 'bout a drink, Mathias.

(MATHIAS turns. JIM is there. He holds the bells.)

MATHIAS. You get out of here, Jim. I did what I could for you. Just got rid of one ghost, I'm not taking up with another.
JIM. Then maybe you better stop killing people.
MATHIAS. Prove it. Nobody can prove it on either you nor the Chinaman. I didn't do anything.
JIM. You killed me, Mathias. Got me drunk, left me out there to freeze.

(JIM goes to the bar, pours them both drinks.)

MATHIAS. You did that yourself, Jim. You got greedy.
JIM. It was a gold rush! Greed was the reason for everything we did.
MATHIAS. Not me. Everything I did, I did for my child.

(MATHIAS pours himself another drink, vaguely desperate. JIM picks up the skull, looks at it.)

JIM. You're wrong. It don't look like nothing. It looks like a man. It looks like us.

(He holds up the skull.)

MATHIAS. You're a figment of my imagination. All of this. My mind running crazy, on a long winter night. The only real danger ever was that Canadian upstairs with all his dreams of justice and redemption. Took care of that, and I took care of you. It's over.

JIM. And your mind? You can take care of that too?
MATHIAS. My mind is my own. So is my will. *(Furious)* My mind, and my will. I did it all. Myself. You'd all be dead if it weren't for me.
JIM. I am dead. So is the Chinaman.
MATHIAS. I'm sick of hearing about that Chinaman! He was nobody! You all didn't think what I did was so godawful that winter when I saved your lives, I saved you— *(The sound of the bells comes up behind him.)* Those goddamn bells!

(ANNETTE, behind him, approaches XUIFEI, who holds the bells.)

ANNETTE. Pa, look!
XUIFEI. Kuh-yi, kuh-yi.

(XUIFEI holds the bells out.)

ANNETTE. What's he saying, Pa?
MATHIAS. I don't know, honey.
XUIFEI. Kuh-yi, hao.

(XUIFEI encourages her to come to him, holding out the bells, showing how they work.)

ANNETTE. Can I do it?
MATHIAS. I can't do this again.
ANNETTE. Can I do it?
XUIFEI. Hao, hun hao.
JIM. I don't see why not.
MATHIAS. *(Reluctant)* Can I get you a drink?

(Friendly, XUIFEI looks up at MATHIAS.)

XUIFEI. Food?
MATHIAS. No, no food. Liquor's all we got.
XUIFEI. Food, I have food.

(He searches through his gear, finds a tin of biscuits, offers it to MATHIAS.)

MATHIAS. Look, you want a drink or not?

(XUIFEI turns to ANNETTE, offers it to her.)

XUIFEI. Bu-yau, bu-yau. Shr-ni-da. Na ba. Na ba.
ANNETTE. What's he saying, Pa?
JIM. Check his money.
MATHIAS. I can't look at this again! It's over and done with!
JIM. Listen to me, Mathias. I heard Stu Campbell's been up there, working a stake up by Fortymile, with some Chinaman. Word is they hit a vein.

(MATHIAS looks over at ANNETTE and XUIFEI. ANNETTE gets the bells to chime.)

ANNETTE. Look, Pa, I'm doing it!
MATHIAS. Look, stranger, I got to ask to see your money. Don't like to do it but it's been a hard winter. Can't serve you unless I see you can pay.
JIM. Me and Charlie working like animals, we didn't end up

with four dollars between us. And he comes in here, a Chinaman, he don't even speak English, and the gold just come out of the earth for him.

(XUIFEI dumps the gold on the table. MATHIAS backs away in horror.)

    MATHIAS. No!
    ANNETTE. Pa, look!
    XUIFEI. *(Offering MATHIAS a piece)* Shr-ni-da. Na ba.
    ANNETTE. What's he saying, Pa?
    MATHIAS. How am I supposed to know?
    XUIFEI. Such a beautiful girl. Will you take this for her? I see in your faces, you are hungry. The outpost up at Fortymile still has supplies. Take this, it is little enough, but it will help.
    MATHIAS. That's not what he said.
    XUIFEI. I am on my way home. Please take this, for the little girl.

(ANNETTE gets the bells going again.)

    ANNETTE. Look, Pa, I can do it!
    MATHIAS. This isn't how it happened.
    CHARLIE. There's an old story, about a prospector. And a bird! And horses committing suicide on the Dead Horse Trail!
    XUIFEI. Do it.

(He holds out the axe.)

    SALLY. Show me your palm, Mathias.

XUIFEI. Do it.
CHARLIE. You're all sons of bitches.

(MATHIAS takes the axe. ANNETTE looks over.)

ANNETTE. What's that, Pa?
XUIFEI. You did it for her. Show her. Show them all.
CHARLIE. One day he wakes up, starts to make himself some coffee, turns around and there's another prospector, heading down the road, moving away from him.
MATHIAS. I am a good man.
XUIFEI. Show her what you did to me.
MATHIAS. What kind of a monster are you?
XUIFEI. You didn't do it for her.
SALLY. Show me your palm.
JIM. He's right, Mathias. I was there. I saw your face. When you saw the gold.
BAPTISTE. The price of the betrayal is not meant to give meaning to the act. The act itself renders the price meaningless.
ANNETTE. Pa?
MATHIAS. She was the price.
BAPTISTE. He was the price!
MATHIAS. Don't listen to them! I am a good man. One moment doesn't make a life!
ANNETTE. What did you do, Pa?
MATHIAS. Your children will be safe!
XUIFEI. My children will never be born.
MATHIAS. I can't care about that! I won't say it. I won't say it for any of you. None of you had the courage to look in your hearts and do what had to be done. You want me to confess! I

won't confess!

SALLY. Show me your palm, Mathias! What is in your palm?

(What is left of the bar flies apart to reveal a lone campfire. The others disappear, leaving XUIFEI, MATHIAS and BAPTISTE on an empty plain, lit only by the light of the campfire.)

BAPTISTE. He gave you a gift as well, that night. To the child he gives the bells. But he sees starvation in her face. So, to you, he gives one piece of gold.

MATHIAS. It isn't enough.

BAPTISTE. No. It isn't. For having seen what you see, only the full amount will do. You see the future. You see ease. Comfort. The solution to all cares. *(XUIFEI takes his pack and goes to sit by the fire.)* You see happiness. You see fulfillment. *(Beat)* You see gold.

(MATHIAS follows XUIFEI, carrying the axe.)

MATHIAS. Chinaman. *(XUIFEI turns, surprised, sees MATHIAS.)* I need the gold. You understand me? The gold in your pack. You're gonna have to give it to me now.

(XUIFEI protests, confused.)

XUIFEI. Wo hwe Jung-guo chu. Jung-guo. Jung-guo.

(MATHIAS takes a step forward, with the axe.)

MATHIAS. I'm not arguing about this! You give it to me, or I'll take it. Give it to me now.

(Frightened, XUIFEI takes the pack and tosses it to MATHIAS.)

XUIFEI. Wo chyou ni. Wo chyou ni.

(MATHIAS looks at it, at his feet.)

MATHIAS. Look away. Look away now.
XUIFEI. *(Protesting, frightened.)* Syansheng, wo chyou chyou ni.

(MATHIAS suddenly grabs him by the shoulder and pushes him down, face forward in the snow. XUIFEI scrambles backwards, frightened.)

MATHIAS. It'll be easier for you if you just lay still.
XUIFEI. *(Begging)* Wo chyou chyou ni! Bu yuah sha sz wo!
MATHIAS. I said look away! *(He raises the axe. XUIFEI holds up his hand to protect his face. MATHIAS brings it down on him. XUIFEI falls to the ground. MATHIAS hits him again, and again. He stops, finally, breathless.)* That wasn't so hard. Just wasn't so hard. *(He hears something in the silence, turns, startled.)* Who's there? No one's there.
BAPTISTE. This far down the trail, no one for miles.
MATHIAS. No one.
BAPTISTE. The prospector, Jim Lynch, he saw you leave the inn. He could, eventually, put the pieces together.
MATHIAS. He'll keep his mouth shut.

BAPTISTE. But what about the body?
MATHIAS. Burn it. Make it look like an abandoned claim. The land is littered with them. Men coming from all the world, looking for gold, finding only the blackened earth. They go home. But the earth is left behind. Just make it look like an abandoned claim.

(He drags the body back to the fire. BAPTISTE watches as he dumps the body, and rests.)

BAPTISTE. And so it is done. You have your heart's desire.
MATHIAS. Yes.
BAPTISTE. The gold. The axe. The fire. It is done. And you are at peace. *(MATHIAS crumples to the ground, wailing from the depths of his grief. BAPTISTE watches for a moment, as XUIFEI rises and stares at MATHIAS.)* You have your treasure.

(He turns upstage and walks away. MATHIAS and XUIFEI consider each other as the earth begins to burn.
Blackout.)

End of play

www.ingramcontent.com/pod-product-compliance
Lightning Source LLC
Chambersburg PA
CBHW051410290426
44108CB00015B/2232